Knock Before

THE CARE PE~~RSONNEL~~

John James BSc (Hons)

Acknowledgements

Firstly, I would like to thank my wife, Lesley, a pure inspiration in my life and the glue that holds me together, I love you. Thank you Monica Marmandiu the most compassionate carer I've ever worked with. Eliza Striunga, for showing me that you can be caring, profession and have fun all at the same time. Thanks, also, to Donna Tauny and Katie Hollis two great managers that truly care about staff and residents. To every externally focussed staff member that I've ever worked with, you are the reason I've been doing this job for so long, thank you. Finally, thank you to every resident I've worked with, you have been my teachers and my inspiration as well as the very heart and soul of what I do.

INTRODUCTION

I have been working in care for thirty plus years both in paid work and as a volunteer; I have a 2.1 honours degree in psychology and qualifications in medication administration and self-harm and suicide prevention. In my career I have worked with learning disabilities, autistic, the homeless, drug addicts, alcoholics, schizophrenics, and dementia. My speciality used to be violent individuals, clients with behaviours that challenge. I began to get too old for the violence, my body couldn't take it and I finally walked away when I got angry, I knew it was time to move on.

As well as many different kinds of clients I have also worked with many different staff, some have been amazing, kind, compassionate, understanding; one staff member I worked with, Monica, was like an angel, I've never seen anyone more gentle. The flip side of that is staff that have been aggressive, selfish, uncaring, inpatient and, yes, abusive.

I've seen staff bring their own baggage into the care environment, staff that openly display their stress, annoyance, grievances and private problems. Staff that have aired those grievances etc to the residents or taken their personal traumas out on residents by becoming short tempered with a resident or treating them like children.

The great carers have been an inspiration. I have learned from all of them and I can honestly say that I am a combination of each great carer that I've had the pleasure and privilege to meet. However, the truly awful carers have also been an inspiration, not only have they been an example of what NOT to do, but they also gave me a reason to write this book. The bad carers as well as the good help me to formulate my ideas, helped me to put together what I call the *Care Personality*.

Within these pages you will see my idea of the Care Personality, a way of being when working in care, from mental preparedness to attitude to behaviour to a psychological state of being. The Care Personality will help you be a better carer for your residents and yourself.

I hope you find the Care Personality useful and you can use the ideas in your own practice, you may not agree with everything I say, in fact, I know a lot of carers and managers with have a problem with some aspects of my ideas, but this is my theory on how one should be in care.

Every single being goes through the same life process, we are born, we age, we get sick, we die. Some are lucky enough to live a long life and not have to be cared for, some are not so lucky.

For those who find themselves in a care facility of some sort, they are cared for to some degree and there are various reasons for them to be there; some have physical impairment, some have mental health issues, emotional instability, are infirm or disease. Whoever it maybe and whatever the reason for them needing support, we, as carers, owe it to every individual to give them the best support we can. We need to work in the service of others in a positive way, picking up the tools of the trade along the way through training and, above all, experience.

There are many ways in which we can support people but at the heart of everything we do from cleaner to laundry, from carer to management and even the owner of the facility, is compassion; without compassion there is no care. So please, as you read on, please know that behind everything I say is the foundation of compassion.

I will use examples throughout this short book. All examples are from my career not a particular care facility. I have tried not to identify the residents or carers, not even by gender by just using the words resident, staff and carer. I do not put myself higher than any carers I mention, I have made many mistakes in my career and I am constantly learning, there will always be more that I don't know than what I do know, but within these pages is my theory of what we should all aspire to be working in care.

For now, thank you for your attention.

PREPARATION

Everyone has their own routine before going to work no matter what job they do, and care is no different. No matter what your routine, wake, shower, breakfast, out the door or shower, breakfast, watch the news, to the car, whatever it maybe, the one thing I believe you must do in care is to get yourself in psychological readiness for the day.

Throughout my career I have seen carers and management enter a care environment with the weight of the world on their shoulders or filled with stress and anxiety. I have witnessed conversations about being *pissed off* at being short staffed or the work that lies ahead. I've heard carers complain about their husbands and wives, having a hangover, having a bad back, hundreds of complaints and gripes. This stress and negativity is then passed on to the residents, whether it be snapping at them if they shout or complain or want attention, or even directly complaining to the resident about the carer being stressed or the team being short staffed, I've even known a carer who was feeling down ask for a hug from a resident to make the carer feel better. The residents are more sensitive to emotions than you realise, your body can tell the residents many things about you. If you are stressed or upset the resident will be aware of this. A tense body, a sharp tone, a sigh of displeasure, are all signs that the resident will see or feel and, maybe unconsciously, react negatively to those signs.

On multiple occasions a resident has remarked to me, "so and so is in a bad mood today," "so, you're short staffed again," "so and so's husband made her cry last night". I don't know why people do this, but this behaviour has no place in care.

You'll find your own way to prepare for the day, I prefer meditation, I chant (as I am of Hindu religion) and I practice deep breathing. Whatever you decide to do you must be in the right headspace, you must be prepared to work in the service of others and leave your 'home self' at the door.

Duality of Thought

When I talk about *duality of thought* I am talking about the two modes of thought that internally focussed carers cling to – Hope and Fear.

Hope is the hope you hold in how you want your day to be, fully staffed, no drama, no problems, maybe that management or a certain staff member aren't in that day.

Fear is the fear of what lies ahead, that you will be short staffed, that the staff member you don't get on with will be on shift with you, that the night staff wouldn't have done that job you asked them to do. The attachment to duality can cause a large amount of stress and even anger sometimes hours before the shift even begins causing harm to your mental and physical health, that stress being passed on to your colleagues and the residents and maybe even affect your home life.

This attachment to duality can be solved by accepting what will be, by understanding that whatever the day holds you will face as we cannot predict what we will encounter. I hear carers screaming, "Easier said than done," and I'm not saying it is easy as I know that attachment to duality, this hope for the best (which rarely works out) and the fear of the worst, is instilled in us especially if we are internally focussed as a person as well as a carer, but our day is not about *us* so much as the resident and do they deserve our stress? No.

My example here comes from when I supported a resident in their own home. Carers had told the relative of the resident that they were stressed because, "they never knew what they'd come into". Not only did this fear of the unknown affect the stress levels of the carer, but that stress was picked up by the resident who then displayed behaviours, a kind of self-fulfilling prophecy that the day did indeed not go well, but also worried and stressed the relative, so your personal stress can affect any number of people.

The day will hold what it holds. A good preparation for work and a positive attitude is essential. You'll hear this again and again as you read on, but we **must** stay externally focussed (more on this below), we must understand that to support the residents is a privilege and to make someone's day brighter is a gift. Yes, caring is hard work, yes, it is poorly paid and, yes, most of the time it may seem a thankless job (more on this later too) but to be internally focussed is a very *me* orientated mode of thinking. Let's look at this more in depth now by examining internal versus external focus.

SEPARATE SELVES

The Care Personality has two modes of working, the Internal Focus and the External Focus. Whichever focus you have will determine the type of carer you will be.

The Internal Focus:

When you work with an Internal Focus you look inward to find the answers. Your decisions will be based on *your* likes, dislikes and *your* thoughts and feelings in that moment. Your behaviour will be reactionary, and your frame of mind will dictate your tone, your body language, your words and your actions. Let me give you some examples that I've witnessed.

As mentioned earlier, the stress you feel can be "passed on" to the residents whether directly or indirectly. I witnessed a carer who seemed highly stressed, she constantly griped about being short staffed and about the work that lay ahead. A resident, with dementia, was constantly shouting. The carer, having enough of the shouting, stormed into the resident's room, *without knocking*, and said, "We can't keep running to you, we have other people to see and we're short staffed".

Another example of Internal Focus happened when all members of staff were on a break *together*, no one was on the floor. A resident pressed the bell, and no one came. I went to see what the resident wanted, the resident said that they were dirty and needed changing. I went and told the carers that the resident wanted changing and the carers said, "We're on our break." The resident had to wait until the carers were finished sitting in their waste for over fifteen minutes.

In both these examples the carers are internally focussed, their stress directed their unacceptable behaviour towards a resident, and their needs, that of a break, came before the desperate needs of the resident.

The internal focus can be changed with training and, sometimes, with experience. The two main types of carers who suffer mostly from internal focus are mostly new carers, as their life patterns are so ingrained into their personality, and long-time carers who are unmotivated, cynical, low morale, bitter and stressed. However, anyone can be internally focussed and it can be learned from the habits of other internally focussed staff. If this type of focus is not rectified then the internally focussed way of working can become the norm.

External Focus:

The carers with external focus look outside of themselves, their focus is on the residents; they work in the service of others, the resident's needs are their primary goal. Carers with external focus can successfully separate their home self and care self. They are focussed on being a positive force and support all the principles of care (more on these soon). If you are externally focussed you are calm, engaging, polite, helpful, understanding and sympathetic.

A prime example of external focus is the carer named Monica that I mentioned earlier. Monica never complained or griped, she spoke softly and calmly and was never flustered. When seeing a resident, she knocked before she entered, her eyes immediately going to the resident and the first thing she did was talk to the resident, "Good morning, how are you?"

Monica was professional in her approach and resident focussed throughout whatever task it was, constantly talking to the resident explaining everything that she was doing or about to do. I worked with Monica with one dementia patient that carers had refused to attend to them because they could be violent. Monica saw past the aggression and all she saw was a resident that needed help. We worked in tandem explaining to the resident as we went and constantly communicated with each other taking various roles to provide a continuity of care. Was the resident violent? Yes. Did we get hit? Yes. Were we successful in our task to clean and redress her? Partially. We managed to get her clean at least. But throughout the task both myself and Monica remained externally focussed.

A resident was shouting, the noise was horrendous, and some carers deliberately avoided going in the room (internal focus), I ventured in and sat next to the bed. The resident was red faced and seemed furious. The resident began to shout at me while the I sat and listened. After a few minutes I began to talk in a very quiet voice, so quiet that the resident had to stop shouting to hear me. As soon as the resident stopped shouting, I began to ask them questions about their life and the resident soon found themselves calm and engaged in conversation, even laughing.

The internal and external focus are not fixed, carers can slip between the two, one day you're a perfectly good carer fully focussed on the resident, another day you may let stress get to you and have internal focus throughout your shift. So how do we stay fixed in the external focus, especially for twelve hours or more? First let us look at some of the principles that help us to work with external focus.

PRINCIPLES OF CARE

There are many ways to talk about the principles of care so I will discuss them in the way I was taught but, as I say, you may find a different list, a more 2020's list, but this is what has work for me for decades.

My way of remembering was taught as an acronym – WE C PRIDER

Working in partnership

Empowerment

Choice

Privacy

Respect

Independence

Dignity

Equality

Rights

If you can, as a carer, support these principles of care then you are working with external focus.

Working in partnership

This means that your external focus is not only for the resident but for relatives, other professionals such as doctors and physio's and your colleagues too. As a carer you will be expected to be able to communicate with people from all walks of life and many professional fields, your training will help some with this, but it is your internal/external focus that will play a major part is how you come across. Some family members will complain or even become aggressive, some may be upset, anxious or confused. Family members have a lot of emotions seeing their relatives and loved ones in a home. You will have to remain calm, respectful and supportive and communicate clearly to those relatives no matter how they act towards you.

Empowerment

Empowerment can be supported by embracing the other principles of care and by giving the resident as much control over their lives as possible. Sometimes the resident will want to relinquish control *even* if they are capable; this 'let others do for me' way of thinking should not be rejected – "No, I'm not helping you, you can do it yourself." This is clearly an internal focus, the carer is irritated that a resident is *taking liberties* or *playing us up* (both phrases I've heard many times from carers). The action of declining to do something they can clearly do should not be the factor that we concentrate on, we should be looking deeper, behind their actions – why are they declining? And it's not because they are a bad or sly person.

Let's look at an example from my career. There was a a resident in their 90's who was capable of moving around with a walker, their mobility was very good for their advanced age. Suddenly, they started to decline to walk without assistance. Some believed that they should be walking that *they did it before therefore they can do it now.* This is internal focus – it takes up more of the carers time, it's another job they have to do. However, if we have an external focus we will not see them declining to walk as an inconvenience but we will look, not at the action itself, but the potential reasons behind their declining. The resident in question had recently had a fall and banged their head, this was not the first fall either, they had suffered numerous falls which led to the suspicion that the resident had lost their confidence and feared yet another fall. I cannot imagine being in that situation, how scared one must feel thinking that you'll fall and hurt yourself again. They may also have been feeling unstable for some time but persevered until they could not walk unaided. Either way, the advanced age catching up or the loss of confidence, is a solid reason why the resident has changed mobility ability. Instead of seeing this as an inconvenience carers must encourage the resident to walk with you there to assist if needed. If the resident continues to decline then the carer should support the resident, record what they observed and report the observation to the nurse who can then organise a re-evaluation of the resident's mobility status. This is external focus.

Choice

This is a basic right but one that carers get wrong all the time. What choices do the residents have, well, simply, every choice we ourselves have. The resident should be able to choose as much as possible in their lives and we should be supporting that, it is written in the mental capacity act that we need to support a residents choices even unwise ones. Let me give a couple of examples.

A resident has a cup of tea every day at 10am. At 10am, the carer prepares the tea and takes it in to the resident. Every day this is done as routine – is this wrong? Yes. It has become so routine that the carer is in automatic mode and makes tea every day, day after day. The choice of the resident is removed, unconsciously maybe, but still removed. What if one day they wanted coffee or milk but were too scared to ask after you'd gone to the trouble of making tea? Every time a drink is made the resident *must* be asked what they would like, even if the answer is tea every time, the choice must be given.

It is the same if a resident needs support to dress, the resident should be given the choice what to wear even if the resident is unable to make a choice by giving them the choice you are working with external focus and supporting the resident how they should be supported, with dignity and respect.

Privacy

It is not only us that need our privacy at times, just because someone lives in a care facility it does not mean that their lives are not private. As carers we cannot give one hundred percent privacy as there is a job to be done, washing, pad changes, feeding, repositioning etc. carers have to enter rooms, but we should give as much privacy as we can.

Giving privacy goes hand in hand with dignity and respect and this means knocking on doors before you enter, now this may sound obvious, however, a lot of carers do not do this. Knocking on the door before entering is one of the first things we learn in care but is one of the first things forgotten, this is because of internal focus; the carer sees themselves as in a place of work so they, unconsciously or knowingly, believe that they have the right just to enter a room as it's their workplace. If you are working with external focus you will understand that the room of a resident is their personal domain and you are a guest as you are when you enter the residence itself. Again, we have to remove the 'me' and the 'I' from our approach.

My example comes from a residential home that I worked in. One of the carers entered a resident's room (without knocking) to put away some clothes in his wardrobe. On entering the room, the resident was in their bed masturbating. The carer rolled their eyes and continued putting the clothes away before leaving. This is shocking in so many ways, but it's how internal focus can completely override any sense of privacy, dignity, respect and independence of the resident – *I have a job to do no matter what.*

Respect

Respect in a care establishment is not earned by the residents, respect is given even if it is not returned. We should not be offended, upset, angry or in anyway take personal anything that the resident does or says. We will cover more about behaviours later. Needless to say, we owe the residents our respect regardless.

A perfect example of respect, and indeed professionalism as a whole, was a care position I held where one of our new residents was admitted with very little personal history, his care needs were recorded but his past was missing. It came to light that the resident had been to prison for the sexual assault of a minor. Now, I understand that this is extremely controversial and a very emotive situation to deal with, especially for those who had children. However, the situation was not handled well by some carers. There was a lot of discussion and some strong opinions, but, at the end of the day, the residents past had nothing to do with the support that we needed to provide. The resident deserved our respect as professionals and our approach should be of external focus, their needs should be met. Our internal focus, our thoughts and emotions on the crime they committed had no part in our approach to the support of the resident.

Independence

The resident should be supported to have as much independence as possible, that is, where possible, supporting freedom of movement around the home, supporting them in activities that they choose to be a part of, giving them space when they require it etc. Again, independence goes hand in hand with dignity and respect. My example this time involved a resident who walked with a walking frame and said that they did not want to use it. The resident had capacity and was told that by walking without their frame they were at a high risk of falling, the resident said that they understood but insisted that they wanted to walk independently of the frame. The warnings have been given and understood and the resident has capacity, therefore they have the right to walk unaided. A carer said that they *had to* use their frame. It was explained that the resident had capacity and had been told of the risks, the carer said, "I don't care, if they fall it's my ass." This is a perfect example of internal focus – the carer was concerned of the personal repercussions if the resident fell. However, remember my earlier remark on the mental health act, we must support a residents decisions, even unwise ones.

If there is any question as to the resident's mental capacity then an assessment must be done but the resident must supported in their decisions, until that assessment is made we must assume capacity of the individual.

Dignity

Our first step towards supporting a residents dignity is, again, knocking on the door before entering a room. I have heard many excuses why knocking on the door was not done from "The resident wouldn't know any different" to "They don't mind, we're friends" to "the door is open, they can see I'm coming in." None of these things are valid. The dignity and respect of the resident *must* be the priority.

Dignity does not end with knocking on doors, shutting the curtains and the door while engaging in personal care, the way you talk and act in their home, treating the residents with respect and courtesy, feeding the resident in the correct manner by giving your full attention to the task and going at the residents speed not your own because "you have a million things to do" and by allowing the resident to take their medication in the manner that they want to such as with juice or water, all together (unless an assessed choking risk) or one at a time. I have witnessed a carer administering medication and telling the resident, "Hurry up, I'm really busy." This short sentence crosses so many lines and is extremely internally focussed – *I'm busy and you must go at my pace so I can get on.* The resident must dictate what we do and how we do it, *we* do not control the situation to suit our agenda.

Equality

Equality is not "treating everyone equally", it is giving everyone the same rights, however, all tasks, the way you act and speak must be person-centred, that is individual depending on the resident and the situation. In one care home I worked at the activity person gave all residents a questionnaire – "what do you wear on your hands in winter?", "what piece of clothing do you wear on your head?", "What do you hear with?" Things of that nature. All residents were given the same questions; however, the staff member did not take into consideration the cognitive ability of individual residents. The questions were challenging for some, who needed prompting to complete them, but one resident had earned two degrees before their tenure in the care home and so got extremely angry to be asked such 'childish questions' (resident's words). Just a little external focus would have prevented the upsetting of the resident and the resulting fall out. Knowing the resident and tailoring your support to meet their individual needs is the only way to true equality.

Rights

Residents have the right to be supported in a manner that follows the above principles of care; they have the right to make decisions, even unwise ones, if they have capacity. Residents have the right to be safe and secure. They have the right to get upset and angry, to swear, to cry and to make reasonable requests from staff and management. All the rights that you and I have, they have. This may seem obvious, but not all carers adhere to this. The example I showed above where the carer told a resident that they *had to* use their walker and other examples throughout my career have seen carers restrict a residents movement (one strapped a resident in a wheelchair all day so that they would not go to the floor without a DoLs), telling residents off for swearing, turning off TV programs that the residents were watching because the *carers* found it offensive. All of these examples are very basic rights of the residents.

Yes, movement can be restricted etc, but only with the correct authority such as the forementioned DoLs (deprivation of liberty) which is there for the protection of all, not just the residents.

The residents are protected under the **Human Rights Act 1998** – Protects the individual in things such as the right to life, protection from discrimination, freedom of thought and religion, freedom from degrading treatment and freedom of expression. **The Care Act 2014** – to provide protection for anyone of age 18 or over in care from abuse and neglect and to ensure good standards of care, **The Mental Capacity Act 2005** – to protect people who may lack the capacity to make their own decisions and provide a legal framework for care representatives to support and empower the resident to make those decisions or make decisions on behalf of the resident.

There are many more ways that the resident's rights are protected, many acts not covered here, it also includes your own in house policies and procedures that will sometimes be resident specific. The residents care plans should be updated on a regular basis to reflect and change in the residents health or their needs, wants and requirements. This is why it is essential that the carers (and management) *know* the residents so that they can identify any changes in the residents so that that they can change their approach and mode of care to suit the resident. All changes that are noticed must also be recorded and reported to ensure the continuity of care.

If you are an externally focussed carer then you will understand and support all the principles of care and as you go about your tasks you will ask yourself – am I doing my best for this resident.

BREAK ON THROUGH

Verbal Communication

With external focus we can communicate in a respectful and calm manner. Our voice will change depending on the situation, but it should always be controlled and appropriate to the resident. Like our actions, our voice should be person-centred. Some residents like upbeat energetic communication whereas others find exaggerated speech or too much excitement irritating. You will find your tone by getting to know your residents.

Your verbal communication will not only be appropriate for the resident but also the situation, you may be upbeat, silly, serious, sympathetic, assertive or compassionate you will move from one tone and verbal approach many times a day, even several times in an hour. Your tone must always be calm and respectful even when faced with aggression. There should be no stress in your voice as this can be picked up by the resident which may affect their mood and/or their behaviour. You must NEVER 'tell off' the resident, be condescending, rude, disrespectful or otherwise negative.

No matter how a resident acts or speaks you must always act, verbally and non-verbally, in an externally focussed way. Outside of the care environment you may react to someone hitting you or shouting at you by retaliation, this is not the same in a care setting. I gave you an example of a stressed member of staff "telling off" a resident about shouting out, well, throughout my career I have seen this internally focussed behaviour literally hundreds of times from a carer refusing to work with a 97 year old resident with dementia because they 'shouted at them' to carers shouting and swearing at a resident when they were verbally aggressive to carers denying a residents rights because it is 'inconvenient' for them to a carer striking a resident because they pinched them. All these examples are unacceptable, internally focussed behaviours. The carers in these examples are responding to a resident by projecting their personal thoughts, feelings and therefore reactions onto the resident.

As previously mentioned, your volume, tone and the emotion in your voice must be person-centred, but also situation-centred. A carer must be adaptable at a minute's notice able to ride the residents emotions and react accordingly in an externally focussed way. This means that an additional skill that is essential to a carer is *active listening*.

An externally focussed approach is to allow the resident time to talk, to say whatever is on their mind and to listen, really listen to what they are saying. Your response to what they are saying is so important for their mental and emotional health. Techniques vary and as mentioned before, you will find what works for you, however, repeating back to the resident what they have said (or the key part of what they said) can show the resident that you are listening and that you understand. You can also show that you are actively listening by making eye contact, nodding to show you understand and responding appropriately. If a resident is upset, your tone must be *sympathetic, understanding and compassionate. The resident may be an emotional person and is constantly upset or easily upset, but this is your time to shine as a carer and your response can bring forth a smile, give comfort, make the residents life happier even if for a little while – this is the pure gold of our job.

*You will notice that I have used the word sympathetic and not empathetic, this is because, controversially maybe, I don't believe that anyone can really put themselves in another person's shoes as everyone's experiences are different. Instead of putting ourselves in their shoes I believe that we should actively listen, be sympathetic and compassionate and just understand how the resident is feeling in the present moment. This, however, is just my opinion.

Finally, it is extremely important to constantly communicate with the resident – speak when you see them about the home, ask how they are, listen and respond to what they say to you. Constant interaction builds trust, improves the residents self-esteem, gives the home a positive, friendly feel and helps the resident feel supported, listened to and cared for. Stay externally focussed, think of the resident, how they feel, how we can improve their life. I know, I'm repeating myself, but it's because I can't say it enough because of the importance of externally focussed care.

Non-Verbal Communication

Like verbal communication, your non-verbal communication (NVC), your body language and facial expressions, must be person and situation centred. Some residents like big dramatic gestures, some do not, some like close proximity, some like their personal space, you need to be able to adapt. There are no hard and fast rules despite what some trainers will tell you and, again, you'll find your way by getting to know your residents. It is, however, essential that your NVC is calm like your verbal communication, non-threatening even in stressful situations (I will talk on challenging behaviour later), friendly, open and appropriate to the situation. As mentioned previously, eye contact is important (unless the client does not like it) and must be synchronised with your voice; by this I mean your body mustn't be saying one thing when your voice is saying something else, for instance, I had a resident say to me that some carers talk to them and she can tell that they are not interested because they are watching TV or "Fiddling with something" (resident's words). Even your facial expressions can affect a resident without you saying a word, you can wear your stress on your face as well as your displeasure, anger or concern so try to be aware of this too.

Your NVC, like verbal communication, must be person centred. Some residents like calm and controlled body language, some don't mind big gestures or excited facial expressions. Some residents like someone to joke with them, banter with them, some prefer a more serious approach. You will discover this as you get to know your resident. Pay attention to their NVC cues to establish the kind of NVC *you* should adapt. Some residents will even tell you, I have been told to, "Calm down," before by a very straightforward resident when I excitedly said *good morning*.

The exceptions to the observations for guidance rule are those who have a problem with NVC such as the physically impaired and those who display challenging behaviour, but even here there will be NVC cues for what they wish to communicate – happiness, pain, I need help, I'm getting annoyed/frustrated. These cues can be identified if you know your residents. You need to pay attention, this will take effort on your part at first but will become second nature.

GHOST IN THE SHELL

Auditory and visual hallucinations are more common than you think in care. I have witnessed hallucinations in those suffering from schizophrenia, autism and dementia. Sometimes the *ghost in the shell*, that is the sights and sounds that go on in people's heads, are sometimes wonderful and bring forth smiles and laughter and sometimes nightmarish that brings forth fear and anxiety.

But what if you, as a carer, encounter a resident that hears or sees things that you don't experience? Well, if you work with an internal focus you will see and hear that there is nothing there, you may even tell the resident, "There's nothing there, it's fine." However, you would be wrong. If a resident is hallucinating then there **is** something there – for the resident. What they see and hear may be very real to them and they may have a strong emotion reaction to what *they* experience. Telling a resident who is hallucinating that there is nothing there, essentially denying their reality, can cause the resident to become fearful and confused, they may think themselves 'mad' or become embarrassed.

If we witness a resident experiencing hallucinations, as always, we must remain externally focussed; we must accept the residents experience as real and walk confidently into their world. First, listen; evaluate what is going on, put your own experiences to one side and pay attention to what the resident is saying about their experience. Secondly, engage. If the hallucination is pleasant then join in, ask questions, join in with the storyline, if your resident seems to be in a field, ask which way they are going, what if we go down this path, can you see any cows. Don't patronise or make fun, just go with it and enjoy the fact that the resident is happy. If the resident find the hallucination distressing then, again, listen to what is being said, get a feel for the problem before you act.

I was once told by a resident that there was a man in their bathroom and he wouldn't leave, the man in the bathroom was a soldier (the resident had been in the army) and was "arguing" with the resident and they wanted the man gone. I walked into the bathroom asking the resident to wait in their room. I "spoke to the man" and asked him to leave. When I exited the bathroom I said that the man had gone and the resident was relieved and settled. On another occasion a resident was shouting at someone that **They** could see while I was trying to talk to the resident. I asked what the matter was and they told me, "He keeps having a go at me, he won't shut up." I told the hallucination, "Look, I'm trying to talk here, either be quiet or leave please." I then turned to the resident and said, "sorry about that, he'll be quiet now." Again, the resident was relieved and settled.

Encountering someone hallucinating when you are new to care may be daunting, even a little scary, so never be afraid to ask for help or advice or talk about what you experienced and get feedback.

HOW CAN I HELP?

One of the most emotional experiences in care is behaviours that challenge. I have seen carers walk away from a challenging situation and never return, carers crying or angry or taking time off with stress, I have had to step away from the job for a few days due to stress, it can be exhausting. In my career, I personally, have been kicked, punched, hair pulled out, spat at and scratched; I spent one Christmas Day in a ten hour restraint and on another occasion was blinded for an hour when a resident fired a fire extinguisher point blank into my face. But it is not just physical aggression that is challenging, as a carer you can be verbally attacked to, shouted at, insulted, called names, your family insulted (my wife has been a target on many occasion).

Let me, in discussing behaviours that challenge, begin with verbal abuse. This, like physical abuse, can come in many forms and many levels of severity. An insult, for instance, "Bitch," should be easy to ignore, but even this one word I have seen trigger an internally focussed carer who took it as a grave insult and turned on the resident and engaged in a prolonged argument. These insults should be ignored but the resident should not.

42

The next step is *being personal.* As previously mentioned my wife has been verbally attacked many times, "Your wife is ugly," "your wife is a bitch." You may be attacked on your looks, called fat, called stupid, have racist comments thrown at you, foul names or sworn at. If things get personal, what do you do? Again, you ignore it. Ignoring something so personal may seem a difficult option but it is the only option, an argument can cause the resident a great deal of distress and escalate the situation that can even reach a physical reaction.

The next stage is verbal aggression, this is beyond insults and moves into anger. This can occur when the resident is in pain or is frustrated. I've seen verbal aggression when a resident is being hoisted, having a dressing changed, when giving personal care, when the resident has a headache and when the resident cannot successfully complete a task, to name a few situations.

Finally, there is threatening verbal aggression. This is aggressive behaviour that makes you feel physically threatened, it may be up close and personal, there maybe threats of physical violence, it may also be accompanied by slamming a fist of a table or throwing something to the floor etc. This can be frightening for some but even in these instances the carer must remain externally focussed. The behaviour should never been seen from the viewpoint of *how does this behaviour affect me*, the verbal abuse should never be the prime focus, the prime focus must always be – Why and how. Why is the behaviour occurring and how can I help the resident. The attack always has a reason, it's never that the resident is bad or nasty, but that the resident needs help and it is your job, as a carer, to help "fix" the problem. Sometimes it may seem that you can't fix the problem, such as if the verbal abuse is through pain from being hoisted, the job has to be done, there's no way around it, but there's always something, it just takes imagination.

I supported a resident who needed hoisting every day and every day they would grow angry, they would swear and shout and call the carers names. I knew from talking to them that they were a Bob Dylan fan, so, as we hoisted them, I began singing Bob Dylan, the resident began to sing along and by the time we had finished the song the hoisting was over and there was no negative behaviours. I began to use this method every time I supported him. Use your knowledge of the resident and think outside the box, it will make your day more pleasant and the resident's life a lot calmer.

When threatened there is your safety to consider and this should always be a priority as well as calming the situation. If a resident is physically threatening and invades your personal space try taking a step back with one foot and turn so that you are sideways on, this way if it did get physical you are a smaller target. Then, raise your hands, palms out and say in a soft calm voice, "we need to calm down so that I can help you. What's the problem?" You say 'we' to remove the personal, that it you are not saying 'you' need to calm which can sound accusatory and apportions blame. The 'how can I help you' let's the resident know that you are there to help so that their cooperation will be beneficial to them. If in doubt then seek advice and/or training from your manager.

In all instances of persistent and/or abusive and aggressive behaviour it MUST be documented. The recording of incidents is not only a legal requirement but allows the nurse to identify patterns of behaviour.

Physical aggression is a regular occurrence in care and again can come in all forms and at varying levels of severity. There is no one way to handle physical aggression but there are many courses out there to teach you techniques, if you feel that you need training then be sure to ask your manager. However, this is where I must warn you about training. I have worked with behaviours that challenge all my career and attended many courses and can honestly say that a basic overview is the best you can ask for. When you are faced with a resident that is physically aggressive it will be very rare to face text book aggression, each individual will have their own personal triggers and behaviours, one resident when angry will not display the same behaviours or in the same way as another so, at risk of repeating myself too much – know your resident.

The thing that we must not do is see these behaviours as bad. As with verbal aggression the behaviours are ways to communicate – I need help, I'm in pain, I need you to understand. We should not concentrate on the behaviours but the reason why the behaviours are occurring. You can also seek advice from your manager or outside agencies if appropriate. Always record the behaviours as this will highlight any patterns in behaviour or pinpoint triggers.

The final thing that I have rarely seen in my career but is one of the most important aspects of behaviours that challenge is the debrief. This seems to be a rare happening, but your manager should be asking how you are when you have been harmed by a resident and measures should be put in place to protect the carer from harm, this may not always be possible as the very fact that you are working with vulnerable people who suffer from conditions that influence behaviour means that sometimes verbal and/or physical aggression is unavoidable.

The two types of behaviours that challenge I have spoken about so far are the two major types that you will encounter, but there are other behaviours that one may find a challenge.

Undressing in public can be embarrassing and frustrating but, as with the behaviours above, look at why the behaviour is occurring rather than the behaviour itself; always stay calm, never get annoyed, always communicate with the person in a calm and respectful way and try to redirect the resident or distract them rather than engaging in confrontation. If others are present you may need to explain to them that everything is fine and the behaviour is not personal. Be prepared to have a sense of humour about these things, a lighter mood will help the situation (without laughing *at* the resident of course). Finally, record all incidents, again, it will be easy to identify patterns of behaviour.

Self-harm is a problem I've only come across a few times in my thirty years and it is a very delicate matter. All instances of self-harm MUST be reported and recorded, even the threat that someone will harm themselves should be reported and recorded. Never confront the person head on about their self-harm but, if you feel confident enough, you can talk to the resident about any problems they are encountering, offer reassurance and let them know that you are there for them.

I supported a resident with severe autism and selective mutism. They would hit themselves with their fist in the sides of the head, so much so that their knuckles bled, the sides of their head were devoid of hair and there were open wounds in the sides of their skull.

One evening, when the wounds were particularly bad, I called the doctor as I was scared for him. The doctor checked him out and prescribed antibiotics but could do little else. The manager was a very internally focussed individual and was angry that I had called the doctor without informing them first.

After much discussion we acquired a DoLs so that the carers could hold his hands to stop him hitting himself. This put the carers in the line of fire, however, the decision meant that the wounds healed and their hair grew back.

One of the behaviours that challenge that I have seen a lot of throughout the years is refusal to take medication. We have to remember that it is the residents right to refuse medication and we must support a residents decision even if it is an unwise one. However, if the resident has been assessed under the mental health act and is found to lack capacity then the manager can apply for a DoLs so that the medication can be given covertly i.e. in a yoghurt.

CARING IS NOT JUST FOR RESIDENTS

The residents must always be your priority but what about your colleagues? Colleagues too will be affected by internally focussed carers. An internally focussed carer will see a difficult day as *their* problem, that *they* are affected by the team being short staffed or by a demanding resident or increased workload, they see each team member as an individual and this puts cooperation in jeopardy from the start. As with everything else we must remain externally focussed when it comes to our fellow colleagues. We are a Team with a capital T and that team needs to look after each other. In my career I have had the privilege of working with some amazing people but also the disadvantage of working with very internally focussed carers.

Take a few minutes to think about what you would like your colleague to be like – maybe hard working, communicative, a sense of humour, logical, positive, thinks outside the box, as well as kind, caring, understanding and patient. However, these people are very rare, so what is your role? Well, you need to be mentor, friend, confidante, leader, follower and a team player. As a carer, as a member of the team you need to be what ever makes the team a strong and cohesive unit. The team must come before yourself. Now, are there people that we don't get on with? Sure, but those thoughts and feelings belong outside with your stress and negativity. The residents and the rest of your team do not deserve to suffer because of personality clashes. If the differences can not be resolved by putting the differences to one side, if for one reason or another the relationship is affecting the team then something needs to be done. Try talking about your problems with the colleague involved, if you feel like you can't then seek some kind of mediation whether that be a willing colleague or management, but the "problem" needs to be solved for the sake of the team and the residents.

I have seen cohesive teams that have also been very poor teams as they were united but united in their negativity, each team member airing their grievances, complaining about conditions or other staff or management, this may unite the team but it destroys morale and affects the residents.

As with the residents we must be there for our team, we do not know what is going on in their lives so we must be understanding and compassionate, do not be afraid to ask if they are okay or to tell them that you are there for them if they need to talk. If you see something that you don't think is right (unless it is serious such as abuse) then talk to your colleague about it, help them to get things right as they should help you. A great team not only helps the day run more smoothly but breeds positivity which in turn helps the residents, everyone benefits.

A GENUINELY OPEN DOOR

A manager should also be externally focussed. Throughout my career I have been the employee of some very internally focussed managers. One of the problems is that care, other than being a compassionate environment to support residents, is a business. This fact causes some managers to become fixated on the business side of the home and this can be all consuming. The running of the home is important but should never come at the cost of compassion.

The manager has a huge responsibility for the *business* but also for the staff and residents. An internally focussed manager will see the staff as names on a rota, as long as the shift is staffed then this is where it ends. The only time that managers talk to their staff is when they feel that they need to be reprimanded. An internally focussed manager will also believe that their word is gospel, that they are the manager and therefore they know best.

An externally focussed manager will know their limits; they will understand that their staff support residents every day and trust that they know their residents. An externally focussed manager will not be afraid to ask a carers thoughts and opinions on residents, this does not show weakness in the manager but strength. Asking a carers opinion shows trust and empowers the carer therefore increasing the carers self-esteem and self-worth and increases morale. The manager should take advantage of the carers experience and knowledge to get things right and help the smooth running of the home. A good manager will be a good communicator and listening is an important part of communication. Being a good communicator also means how you speak to your staff, they must be treated with kindness and respect and never spoken down to. As with staff, any stress, irritation or general bad mood must not be reflected in how you talk to staff or interact with them. The standards that you ask from you staff must be the same standards that you embody yourself.

Let us look at some scenarios that a manager may find themselves in with staff and look at how an externally focussed manager should present themselves.

Individual interaction: the manager may have to change their tone depending on the situation, but in general must always be polite and friendly; if there has been a complaint against the staff member the tone must be non-accusatory, the staff member must be *asked* about the complaint not spoken down to as if the complaint is automatically true.   Here is an example of how the conversation should begin, *"We've received a complaint about you from another staff member, they say that you swore at a resident, what's your take on it?"* As you can see, the manager in this example has given the employee the complaint but has not assumed that it is true, there could be a miscommunication of some kind that has led to the complaint, this approach gives the employee the chance to explain.

If something serious needs to be emphasised, the tone must be firm, even assertive but, again, always respectful, even if the employee's tone is negative or aggressive, the manager must always be in control of their own tone and remain professional. A manager must never raise their voice to an employee remaining calm and dignified at all times.

Supervision: in a supervision, the internally focussed manager will use it as a platform to air all grievances or complaints, to point out supposed faults of the staff member. However, a supervision is the staff members time and must be used to support their self-esteem and motivate them, therefore, if there are points that the manager needs to make, that may seem negative to the employee, then this must be sandwiched between positives. A staff members positive qualities should be emphasised, and praise given for hard work and points such as flexibility, teamwork or positive attitude. The staff member must leave a supervision feeling good, leaving feeling bad can lower morale and in return the residents will suffer.

Staff meeting: staff meetings are important to give information to everyone at the same time but, like supervisions, the meeting should start and end with a positive. If a staff meeting is used as a group *telling off* or ends with a negative comment the staff go way feeling demoralised and negative which can lead to a less productive day. Thank the staff for their hard work and commitment but do this at the end of the meeting, let it be the last thing your staff hear, not complaining.

In 1885 German psychologist, Hermann Ebbinghaus, pioneered the *Serial Position Effect* that suggested that our memories are more likely to remember the first thing that was said (primacy effect) and the last thing (the recency effect); applying this model to the staff meeting, if the meeting begins and ends with a positive then these are the things that stay in our minds at the end of the meeting and therefore leave the employee with a positive feeling.

The points above are extremely important for staff morale. I have worked under managers that constantly complain about low staff morale without realising that it starts at the top. If a staff team sees a manager who is motivated, caring and understanding they see them as a manager that the staff can "get on board with".

Tips for a manager:

- Try walking around the home in a morning and saying good morning to all the staff.
- Walk around before you leave and thank the staff for the day.
- Know the residents, it's not only the staff that need to know the residents, as the manager they are under your care so talk to the residents, wish them happy birthday or happy anniversary and get to know them as people.
- Trust your staff. Their opinion is based on time with the residents.
- Be a manager not a tyrant. The "my decision is final because I'm the boss" attitude can be antagonistic.
- Praise good work and find the positive in any situation. Only calling a meeting with a staff

member to complain about a mistake is counterproductive. Praise, don't just criticise.

- Say, "Thank you," those two words can lift a staff member more than you know.
- Remember, people make mistakes, we are all human.
- Be proactive not *reactive*. Don't let past events or your own perceptions influence your decision making, face each challenge as it comes, be open to new ideas and think long term.

A manager is a leader, a mentor, an inspiration, a driving force behind the staff team. Their job is multifaceted but the human side of their job can get lost in the business side of things if you let it. The responsibility is enormous, and this should be, and must be, understood by the staff, but a manager has to engage with the human aspect of their job as without staff there would be no business, without residents there would be no business. Their door must always be open (metaphorically) and not just a phrase one repeats but a **genuinely** open door.

Throughout my career I have worked with many managers, some have been extremely internally focussed, their mind has been purely business with no concept of humanity. They have been abrasive, dismissive and condescending with a superior attitude that bred a negative atmosphere and made working uncomfortable. However, I have worked with some inspirational managers who really care about staff and residents, they have been positive, compassionate, understanding, trusting, even fun, which bred a very positive atmosphere and made coming to work a joy. Be the latter.

INSPECTOR TERRIFIER

They appear from nowhere and demand access to your home and your records, they watch your staff and test them by asking about safeguarding and mental capacity etc…they are **The Inspectors**.

Whenever the phrase, *the inspectors are coming*, is uttered in a care home the whole organisation seems to panic, but why? The reason for panic is simple, the inspectors may see something that should not be happening. However, the inspector's visit should be viewed as **a.** a learning experience as they may find something that we as a team did not see that could be improved and **b.** as a way to showcase the home because everything should be in place, every staff member should know their job and all records should be up to date and correct. "You live in a fantasy world!" I hear you cry, yes, this may be, but I'm serious. I understand that not everything goes to plan but most things should be in place and with externally focussed staff and management a care home should welcome inspectors.

The CQC (Care Quality Commission), for instance, look at whether the residents are safe and if they are treated with compassion, dignity and respect; are organisations meeting people's needs in a person-centred way and are the residents free from neglect, inappropriate limits on freedom, abuse of any kind or unnecessary or inappropriate restraint; they make sure that staff numbers are sufficient, that the premises and equipment are fit for service and that the management and the organisation are providing high-quality care. Which of these standards should not be automatically provided? Which of these standards is not achievable? The answer should be none. These standards are the standards of basic human need and with external focus these standards would be met as a matter of course. The CQC should be walking away with a satisfied grin.

If this is not the case then a manager should ask themselves why the standard is not being met and approach the problems in a calm and methodical manner, not by bullying the staff by constant complaining, but by leading from the front and encouraging the staff to up their game.

THE WAY FORWARD

So, how do we ensure an externally focussed staff team? Well, it begins with the staff selection. I mentioned earlier that in some cases staff are just names on rotas and as long as the shift is covered then that's fine and the same can be said for some new employees, the fact that staff positions need to be filled can be a reason to take just anyone on, this should never be the case. Any employee should be interviewed in a rigorous manner, testing not only their knowledge, but their personality, attitude and social skills. We need to remember that the staff are supporting vulnerable people with needs and we need the best people to provide that service and not only carers but domestics, kitchen staff, office staff, activities and maintenance, everyone should meet a high standard for the sake of the residents.

The next step is the management. Leadership, as I stated earlier, is so important, it is the engine of the ship that propels it on its journey. A great manager will use all the skills listed above to motivate and inspire the team to provide the best care possible.

The staff need to take responsibility and remain externally focussed. Employees must ensure positivity even when short staffed or with a difficult resident. We have to understand that we are a guest in the resident's home and to help make people's lives better is such a privilege. Only when we put aside our 'me' and 'I' can we be externally focussed and excel in the service of others.

I have been working in care for 30+ years and I love it more now than ever. I am not perfect, I make mistakes, I say the wrong thing, I can be negative and lose focus, but the key is to acknowledge that, to not let a mistake destroy you, to live without ego and ask for help if needed and take responsibility and accountability. The residents need and deserve the best care we can provide and every kind word and smile helps and at the heart of everything you do must be compassion.

FINAL THOUGHTS

When reading my theory on care – The Care Personality – you may think that, in many cases, I am stating the obvious, of course we should be kind and compassionate and respectful etc. Well, what I'm suggesting may seem like the simplest thing in the world and, indeed, it is, yet in my career of decades working in care I have seen the simplest things ignored and if we ignore the little things how can we be expected to get the big things right? We may not see not knocking on a residents door before we enter as something to worry about, but this is a sign of respect, privacy and dignity, if we ignore this then where does it go from there?

If we look at an extreme example from my career, I, and others, reported carers leaving cleaning items in a resident's room, this was ignored on the first and second time it was reported. One summers day a carer had left a bottle of clear cleaning fluid in a resident's room, the resident, thinking it was water, drank it and 999 had to be called.

The small things matter.

I end on a positive. I once worked with a resident who was severely autistic, non-verbal, could not read or write or tell you in any way what he wanted. I worked with him as his keyworker. His biggest challenge was wanting to go to the toilet, he could not indicate when he wanted to go and this led to a few accidents. Every day, several times a day, I signed 'toilet' to him, explaining what it meant, over and over again, I never gave up trying. Two years later he signed toilet to me signing that he wanted to go – two years! You could not believe how happy I was. I ran to my manager literally jumping up and down, when I told her she joined me leaping out of her chair, we hugged and cheered.

The small things matter.

Printed in Great Britain
by Amazon

20496642R00041